HYMNS of EXALTATION

8 Piano and Vocal Hymn Arrangements
Late Intermediate - Advanced Piano Solos

Music Mentor

JERALD SIMON

Learn how to play piano the FUN way!
The Apprentice Stage™ - The Maestro Stage™ - The Virtuoso Stage™

Music Motivation®
musicmotivation.com
Music that excites, entertains, and educates! ™

Music Motivation® books are designed to provide students with music instruction that will enable them to improve and increase their successes in the field of music. It is also intended to enhance appreciation and understanding of various styles of music from classical to jazz, blues, rock, popular, new age, hymns, and more. The author and publisher disclaim any liability or accountability for the misuse of this material as it was intended by the author.

I hope you enjoy **"Hymns of Exaltation"** I am excited to have you play these piano and vocal hymn arrangements.

The piano music is perfect for piano students, advanced pianists, piano teachers, and anyone who wants to play or sing these beautiful and well loved hymns. These are late intermediate to advanced level piano pieces. You can listen to the music for the pieces from this book on my website, musicmotivation.com, and also on my YouTube channel - YouTube.com/jeraldsimon.

I hope you enjoy learning about this and all of my other music books! You can learn more at musicmotivation.com, http://essentialpianoexercises.com, and essentialpianolessons.com.

Your Music Mentor, Jerald Simon

This book is dedicated to my children - my daughter **Summer**, and my sons **Preston**, and **Matthew** - with a special thank you for my beautiful wife, **Suzanne (Zanny)**. I love you! I hope you all continually do your best in all you do! You can accomplish anything you set out to accomplish. Imagine the kind of world you would like to create and go about creating it. It is also for the many piano students enrolled in my **Essential Piano Exercises Course** (http://essentialpianoexercises.com).

I create these books from this series for all of you!

CONNECT with Jerald

https://www.musicmotivation.com/jeraldsimon
https://www.facebook.com/jeraldsimon/
https://www.youtube.com/jeraldsimon
https://www.linkedin.com/in/jeraldsimon/
https://www.pinterest.com/jeraldsimon/
https://twitter.com/jeraldsimon
https://www.instagram.com/jeraldsimon/
jeraldsimon@musicmotivation.com

CONTACT Music Motivation

Music Motivation®
Cool music that excites, entertains, and educates!

Music Motivation®
P.O. Box 910005
St. George, UT 84791-0005
https://www.musicmotivation.com/
https://www.facebook.com/musicmotivation
https://twitter.com/musicmotivation
info@musicmotivation.com

First Printing 2009 - Printed in the United States of America - 10 9 8 7 6 5 4 3 - Simon, Jerald - Music Motivation® - Hymns of Exaltation - $20.95 US/ $22.95 Canada - Paperback book - ISBN-13: 978-0-9790716-5-2; Music Motivation Cataloging: MM00001007 (Updated and revised 2023)

Music Motivation® is a registered ® trademark

Music Motivation® - https://www.musicmotivation.com

Welcome to "Hymns of Exaltation" by JERALD SIMON

Piano teachers, piano students, and parents of piano students continually search for fun and exciting piano music their students can't wait to play.

The search is over with Music Motivation® and the music composed by Jerald Simon!

Jerald Simon is a popular pianist, composer, author, and performer/motivational speaker, who composes fun piano music that piano students love playing and performing for family and friends. Simon is well known for his **COOL SONGS Series** (https://www.musicmotivation. com/coolsongs) which features over 200 of his fun, original piano music - most of which include accompaniment MP3 minus tracks to help piano students learn to play the piano the fun way. He is also well known for his **Essential Piano Exercises Series** (https://www. essentialpianoexercises.com/pdf/series), as well as his popular Music Motivation® website and company (https://www.musicmotivation.com/).

In "Hymns of Exaltation," Simon has arranged 8 well known and loved hymns for late intermediate - advanced levels that range in style from contemporary, classical, and new age, to a cinematic, score-like sound. This 72 page book includes all of the lyrics so performers can sing along with the accompaniment. You will enjoy playing and singing these hymns as you have never heard them performed like this before.

It is the hope of the author and publisher that each of these hymn arrangements will uplift, inspire, comfort, and empower the performers and listeners. Hymns are magnificent because they help us focus on that which is of most worth to us. As we listen to the melodies, we think of the inspired words of the hymn.

The order of the hymn selections in this book has a deliberate order. As we look at the beauty of this earth, our souls are stilled. We have imperfections, but we strive to be nearer to God. By doing so, we stand amazed and ask God to abide with us. We need Him and His light in our lives because He gives us more holiness. We hear His voice and come to Him because He loves us and we are His.

I'd like to introduce myself and tell you more about myself and why I love composing fun music to help motivate teens and adults.

My name is Jerald Simon. First and foremost, I am a husband to my beautiful wife, Zanny (her name is Suzanne - but anyone who knows her calls her Zanny), and a father to my three wonderful children, Summer, Preston, and Matthew. They are wonderful, and everything I do is for them. God and family always comes first in my life!

I am the founder of **Music Motivation®** (musicmotivation.com), and the creator of the Cool Songs Series (musicmotivation.com/coolsongs), and the Essential Piano Exercises Series/ Course (essentialpianoexercises.com). I teach weekly online group piano lessons to students all over the world (essentialpianolessons.com). I have a YouTube channel (youtube.com/ jeraldsimon), and I love learning everything I can, and want to help myself and others do our best and live our best life.

Be sure to check out Jerald's **BEST-SELLING** piano book series: **Essential Piano Exercises Every Piano Player Should Know.** There are currently four books in the series. Other books in this series will soon be available as well (e.g. **Essential Pop Piano Exercises Every Piano Player Should Know, Essential Rock Piano Exercises Every Piano Player Should Know, 100 Chord Progressions Every Piano Player Should Know, 100 Improvised Licks Every Piano Player Should Know,** and so forth).

The four books currently in the series are:

"**100 Left Hand Patterns Every Piano Player Should Know,**" "**Essential Piano Exercises Every Piano Player Should Know,**" "**Essential Jazz Piano Exercises Every Piano Player Should Know,**" and "**Essential New Age Piano Exercises Every Piano Player Should Know.**"

You can learn more about these books from the Essential Piano Exercises Series and learn more about the course which you can sign up for at https://www.essentialpianoexercises.com/. The Essential Piano Exercises Series teaches fun exercises through original music I have composed.

A message from Jerald to piano students and parents:

If you come to piano lessons each week and walk away only having learned about music notation, rhythm, and dots on a page, then I have failed as a Music Mentor. Life lessons are just as important, if not more important than music lessons. I would rather have you learn more about goal setting and achieving, character, dedication, and personal improvement. To have you learn to love music, appreciate it, and play it, is a wonderful byproduct you will have for the rest of your life - a talent that will enrich your life and the lives of others. To become a better musician is wonderful and important, but to become a better person is more important.

As a Music Mentor I want to mentor students to be the very best they can be. If you choose not to practice, you essentially choose not to improve. This is true in any area of life. Everyone has the same amount of time allotted to them. What you choose to do with your time, and where you spend your time, has little to do with the activities being done and more to do with the value attached to each activity.

I believe it's important to be well-rounded and have many diverse interests. I want students to enjoy music, to learn to be creative and understand how to express themselves musically - either by creating music of their own, or interpreting the music of others - by arranging and improvising well known music. In addition, I encourage students to play sports, dance, sing, draw, read, and develop all of their talents. I want them to be more than musicians, I want them to learn to become well-rounded individuals.

Above all, I want everyone to continually improve and do their best. I encourage everyone to set goals, dream big, and be the best they can be in whatever they choose to do. Life is full of wonderful choices. Choose the best out of life and learn as much as you can from everyone everywhere. I prefer being called a Music Mentor because I want to mentor others and help them to live their dreams.

Your life is your musical symphony. Make it a masterpiece!

Music Mentor
JERALD SIMON

Music Motivation® - https://www.musicmotivation.com

Learn about my three stages of music success from my **Music Mentorship Map** below -
The Apprentice Stage™, **The Maestro Stage™**, and **The Virtuoso Stage™**
https://www.essentialpianolessons.com

The *Music Motivation®* Mentorship Map (for piano students)
by Music Mentor™ Jerald Simon

Music Motivation®
musicmotivation.com

	🎵 **Apprentice** 🎵 for 1st & 2nd year students	🎵 **Maestro** 🎵 for 2nd - 4th year students	🎵 **Virtuoso** 🎵 for 3rd year students and above
Repertoire In addition to the books listed to the right, students can sign up to receive the weekly "Cool Song" and "Cool Exercise" composed by Jerald Simon every week. Visit musicmotivation.com annual subscription to learn more and sign up!	**Music Motivation® Book(s)** What Every Pianist Should Know (Free PDF) Essential Piano Exercises (section 1) Cool Songs for Cool Kids (pre-primer level) Cool Songs for Cool Kids (primer level) Cool Songs for Cool Kids (book 1) The Pentascale Pop Star (books 1 and 2) Songs in Pentascale position: Classical, Jazz, Blues, Popular, Students Choice, Personal Composition (in pentascale position - 5 note piano solo) etc.	**Music Motivation® Book(s)** Essential Piano Exercises (section 2) An Introduction to Scales and Modes Cool Songs for Cool Kids (book 2) Cool Songs for Cool Kids (book 3) Variations on Mary Had a Little Lamb Twinkle Those Stars, Jazzed about Christmas, Jazzed about 4th of July Baroque, Romantic, Classical, Jazz, Blues, Popular, New Age, Student's Choice, Personal Composition.	**Music Motivation® Book(s)** Essential Piano Exercises (section 3) Cool Songs that ROCK! (books 1 & 2) Triumphant, Sea Fever, Sweet Melancholy, The Dawn of a New Age, Sweet Modality, Jazzed about Jazz, Jazzed about Classical Music, Jingle Those Bells, Cinematic Solos, Hymn Arranging Baroque, Romantic, Classical, Jazz, Blues, Popular, New Age, Contemporary, Broadway Show Tunes, Standards, Student's Choice, Personal Composition
Music Terminology	Piano (*p*), Forte (*f*) Mezzo Piano (*mp*) Mezzo Forte (*mf*) Pianissimo (*pp*) Fortissimo (*ff*) *Music Motivation® 1st Year Terminology*	Tempo Markings Dynamic Markings Parts of the Piano Styles and Genres of Music *Music Motivation® 2nd Year Terminology*	Pocket Music Dictionary (2 - 3 years) Harvard Dictionary of Music (4 + years) Parts/History of the Piano Music Composers (Weekly Biographies) *Music Motivation® 3rd Year Terminology*
Key Signatures	C, G, D, A, F, B♭, E♭ & A♭ (Major) A, E, B, F♯, D, G, C & F (Minor) Begin learning all major key signatures	Circle of 5ths/Circle of 4ths All Major and Minor key signatures (Identify each key and name the sharps and flats)	Spiral of Fifths, Chord Progressions within Key Signatures. Modulating from one Key Signature to another.
Music Notation	Names and Positions of notes on the staff (both hands - Treble and Bass Clefs)	Names and Positions of notes above and below the staff (both hands)	History of Music Notation (the development of notation), Monks & Music, Gregorian Chants, Music changes over the years and how music has changed. Learn **Finale** and **Logic Pro** (notate your music)
Rhythms	Whole notes/rests (say it and play it - count out loud) Half notes/rests (say it and play it - count out loud) Quarter notes/rests (say it and play it - count out loud) Eighth notes/rests (say it and play it - count out loud)	Sixteenth notes/rests (say it and play it - count out loud) Thirty-second notes/rests (say it and play it - count out loud) Sixty-fourth notes/rests (say it and play it - count out loud)	One-hundred-twenty-eighth notes/rests For more on rhythm, I recommend: "Rhythmic Training" by Robert Starer and "Logical Approach to Rhythmic Notation" (books 1 & 2) by Phil Perkins
Intervals	1st, 2nd, 3rd, 4th, 5th, 6th, 7th, 8th, and 9th intervals (key of C, G, D, F, B♭, and E♭). Harmonic and Melodic intervals (key of C, G, D, A, E, and B)	All Perfect, Major, Minor, Augmented, and Diminished intervals (in every key) All Harmonic and Melodic intervals Explain the intervals used to create major, minor, diminished, and augmented chords?	9th, 11th, and 13th intervals Analyze music (Hymns and Classical) to identify intervals used in each measure. Identify/Name intervals used in chords.
Scales	All Major Pentascales (5 finger scale) All Minor Pentascales (5 finger scale) All Diminished Pentascales (5 finger scale) C Major Scale (1 octave) A min. Scale (1 oct.) (Do, Re, Mi, Fa, Sol, La, Ti, Do) (solfege) All Major and Natural Minor Scales - 1 octave	All Major Scales (Every Key 1 - 2 octaves) All Minor Scales (Every Key 1 - 2 octaves) (natural, harmonic, and melodic minor scales) (Do, Di, Re, Ri, Mi, Fa, Fi, Sol, Si, La, Li, Ti, Do) (solfege - chromatic)	All Major Scales (Every Key 3 - 5 Octaves) All Minor Scales (Every Key 3 - 5 Octaves) All Blues Scales (major and minor) Cultural Scales (25 + scales)
Modes	Ionian/Aeolian (C/A, G/E, D/B, A/F♯)	All Modes (I, D, P, L, M, A, L) All keys	Modulating with the Modes (Dorian to Dorian)
Chords	All Major Chords, All Minor Chords, All Diminished Chords, C Sus 2, C Sus 4, C+ (Aug.), C 6th, C minor 6th, C 7th, C Maj. 7th, C minor Major 7th, A min., A Sus 2, A Sus 4,	All Major, Minor, Diminished, Augmented, Sus 2, Sus 4, Sixth, Minor Sixth, Dominant 7th and Major 7th Chords	Review All Chords from 1st and 2nd year experiences All 7th, 9th, 11th, and 13th chords inversions and voicings.
Arpeggios	Same chords as above (1 - 2 octaves)	Same chords as above (3 - 4 octaves)	Same chords as above (4 + octaves)
Inversions	Same chords as above (1 - 2 octaves)	Same chords as above (3 - 4 octaves)	Same chords as above (4 + octaves)
Technique (other)	Schmitt Preparatory Exercises, (Hanon)	Wieck, Hanon, Bach (well tempered clavier)	Bertini-Germer, Czerny, I. Philipp
Sight Reading	Key of C Major and G Major	Key of C, G, D, A, E, F, B♭, E♭, A♭, D♭	All Key Signatures, Hymns, Classical
Ear Training	Major versus Minor sounds (chords/intervals)	C, D, E, F, G, A, B, and intervals	Key Signatures and Chords, Play w/ IPod
Music History	The origins of the Piano Forte	Baroque, Classical, Jazz, Blues	Students choice - All genres, Composers
Improvisation	Mary Had a Little Lamb, Twinkle, Twinkle...	Blues Pentascale, Barrelhouse Blues	Classical, New Age, Jazz, Blues, etc. Play w/ IPod
Composition	5 note melody (both hands - key of C and G)	One - Two Page Song (include key change)	Lyrical, Classical, New Age, Jazz, etc.

"For the Beauty of the Earth" has been written in the key of G major. Play the G major scale below.

	G	A	B	C	D	E	F#	G
	M	m	m	M	M	M	m	d°	M

M represents Major Chords

m represents minor Chords

d° represents diminished Chords

Once you feel comfortable playing the G major scale up and down one octave, try playing it 2, 3, and 4 octaves up and down the piano. As a fun exercise, try playing all of the scales and chords in every key signature by moving up in half steps to the right.

For the Beauty of the Earth is in the key of G Major. The piece features octave chords and intervals.

At the end of every verse, the words of the hymn repeat the phrase: "Lord of all, to Thee we raise, this our hymn of grateful praise." At the end of every verse in this instrumental arrangement I have done, I chose to create my own musical version of a "hymn of grateful praise." After trying this example and playing the entire song, see if you can create your own "hymn of grateful praise" as well.

The example to the left shows measures 57 - 58 from this arrangement. As you play throught this song, you will notice that measures 57 - 64 have a different feeling than the rest of the hymn. I intentionally decided to create a rubato-like free flowing quality with this section. You will also notice a lot of syncopation and off beat rythmns that create an almost lyrical or dance-like movement with the music. This section can be a little more challenging to learn because it changes the overall feeling of the piece quickly before returning back to the moving octave chords.

FOR THE BEAUTY OF THE EARTH

Music by Conrad Kocher, 1786-1872
Text by Folliott S. Pierpoint, 1835-1917
ARR. BY JERALD SIMON

This can also be performed by a female voice. Sing it in your vocal range.

Beautifully (♩ = c. 65-70)

Pedal ad lib. throughout

Lyrics (measure 11):
For the beau-ty of the earth, For the beau-ty of the skies,

For the love which from our birth
O - ver and a - round us lies

Lord of all to thee we raise
This our hymn of grate - ful _____

Energetically (♩ = c. 115 - 118)

praise. _____

For the _____ beau - ty _____ of each hour

Of the ____ day ____ and ____ of the night, _____

_____ Hill and vale, and tree and

39
G7
C7
D7/C
Cadd2
flow'r, Sun and moon, and
42
Gsus
Gadd2
D/G
Emin7
D/F♯
stars of light, Lord of all to
46
C/G
Gm7♯5
Cm7♯5
D7/C
Cadd2
thee we raise This our hymn of

Lyrics:
grate - - - ful praise.

For the joy of hu - man love, Bro - ther, and sis - ter, and

Lyrics:
par - ent ___ and child, Friends on earth, and

friends a - bove, For all ___ gen - - tle

thoughts ___ and mild, Lord of ___

78
D/F♯
C/G
Gm9♯5
Cm9♯5
D7/C
Cadd2
all to thee we raise
This our hymn
82
Gadd2/D
D7
G/D
D
G
of grate - - - - ful
praise.
rit.
a tempo
87
GsusM9
Emin7
D9/E
G/C

Beautifully (♩ = c. 86)
91
Dsus7
D7
G
C/G
G
For the beau - ty of the earth,
rit.
mp
Energetically (♩ = c. 115 - 118)
97
G/C
D
G/D
D
G
GsusM9
This will be our hymn of grate - ful praise.
f
a tempo
102
G
GsusM9
G
8va
15ma
rit.

"Be Still My Soul" has been written in the key of F major. Play the F major scale below.

Once you feel comfortable playing the F major scale up and down one octave, try playing it 2, 3, and 4 octaves up and down the piano. As a fun exercise, try playing all of the scales and chords in every key signature by moving up in half steps to the right.

Ⓜ represents Major Chords

m   represents minor Chords

d° represents diminished Chords

Since the title is "Be Still, My Soul," I wanted to begin the arrangement in the minor key signature as if the soul had not yet been stilled. The tense minor feeling persists until the second verse begins, when the soul finally finds comfort and peace.

The first verse of "Be Still My Soul" has been written in the key of D minor, which is the relative minor of F Major (D E F G A B flat C D). Play the D harmnonic minor scale below (D E F G A B flat C sharp D).

The D harmonic minor scale has a C sharp (the 7th interval has been raised half a step).

Once you feel comfortable playing the D minor scale up and down one octave, try playing it 2, 3, and 4 octaves up and down the piano. As a fun exercise, try playing all of the minor scales and chords in every key signature by moving up in half steps to the right.

Ⓜ represents Major Chords

m   represents minor Chords

d° represents diminished Chords

Aug+ represents augmented Chords

The first measure above shows the D harmonic minor scale. It is different than the natural or relative minor scale because in the harmonic minor scale, the 7th note of the scale is raised up (to the right) half a step. In the case of the D relative minor scale (D E F G A B flat C D) the 7th is a natural and is not sharped. With the harmonic minor scale, the C is raised up half a step and becomes C sharp. Every minor scale in every key signature follows this chord progression of minor - diminished - augmented - minor - Major - Major - diminished - minor. For fun, try playing every major scale one, two, three, and four octaves up and down the piano. You can also try to play every relative and harmonic minor scale up and down the piano one, two, three, and four octaves as well. Have fun with it. This will really help you improve your piano playing.

Be Still My Soul

Music by Jean Sibelius, 1865-1957
Text by Katharina von Schlegel, b. 1697
ARR. BY JERALD SIMON

This can also be performed by a female voice. Sing it in your vocal range.

Filled with sorrow ♩ = 65-70

Be still, my soul: The Lord is on thy side; ___

With pa-tience bear thy cross of grief or pain. Leave to thy

God ___ to or-der and pro-vide; In ev-'ry change he

Pedal ad lib. throughout

17
B♭sus2 C/G A C/F Dm
faith-ful will re - main. Be still, my soul: Thy
8va
mf
23
F/B♭ Am7 Csus9/G Gm9 D7/A Gm7/B♭ F/C F/C C9sus4 C7
best, they heav'n - ly Friend Thru thorn - y ways leads to a joy - ful
f
28
Fm7♯5 B♭sus2 F B♭sus2 C7 F
end. Be still, my
mp
sweetly
crescendo

Lyrics (vocal line):

m. 33: soul: Thy God doth un - der - take___ To guide the fu - ture

m. 38: as he has the past. Thy hope, thy con - fi - dence let noth-ing-ing shake;

m. 44: All now mys - te - rious shall be bright at last. Be still, my soul:___ The

Chord symbols:

m. 33: B♭ — C/F — C7 F — B♭sus2

m. 38: C/F F B♭add2 — F — C/F F/B♭ B♭M9 — Dm7 Am7 — G min

m. 44: G m G♭dim/A F/C — F/B♭ C — F — B♭M7

Dynamics/markings: mf, rit., a tempo

Music Motivation® - https://www.musicmotivation.com

50
Am7 Am7/E Dm7♯5 B♭add2 Fm7♯5 Gm9 D7/A Gm7/B♭ F/C
waves and winds still know His voice who ruled them
p
f
8vb
54
C9sus4 C7 Fm7♯5 B♭add2 F B♭add2
while he dwelt be-low.
mp
sweetly
Powerfully (♩= c. 70 - 90) (as if overcome with immense joy)
59
F♯ Badd2/F♯ Badd2 F♯
Be still, my soul: The hour is
f

has - t'ning on_____ When we shall be   for - ev - er

with   the Lord,   When dis - ap - point - ment,   grief, and fear are gone,

Sor - rows for - got,_____ love's pur - est joys re stored.   Be still, my

Lyrics:

soul: When change and tears are past, All safe and bless - ed we shall meet at

last. _____

"Nearer My God to Thee" has been written in the key of F major. Play the F major scale below.

Once you feel comfortable playing the F major scale up and down one octave, try playing it 2, 3, and 4 octaves up and down the piano. As a fun exercise, try playing all of the scales and chords in every key signature by moving up in half steps to the right.

(M) represents Major Chords

m represents minor Chords

d° represents diminished Chords

Try this rhythm pattern. The left and right hand rhythms are very different from the original hymn.

This arrangement is meant to be moving (literally) because the right and left hands move up and down the keys. The progression basically follows the F major scale. I did this to create an auditory effect of moving nearer to God as we ascend the scale. Play the following example from the piece:

There is a key change after the second verse. The song changes to the key of G major (everything has been taken up 1 whole step). As a review, play the G major scale from "For the Beauty of the Earth." For fun, play your favorite hymn as it is, and then try to change keys by moving up half a step or a whole step to the right. It's a fun exercise and you will learn a great deal about changing keys. If you're in the key of C, pretend the song is in the key of C sharp. You will play the exact same notes on the page, but in your mind, you will need to think of every note as a sharp. C becomes C sharp, D becomes D sharp, and so forth. It adds so much depth and movement to the song when you change keys. Go for it. Try it! Change things up a little with your own piano playing.

NEARER, MY GOD TO THEE

Music by Lowell Mason, 1792-1872
Text by Sarah F. Adams, 1805-1848
ARR. BY JERALD SIMON

14
B♭add2
F/C
C
C7
F
God, to thee, Near - er to thee!
mf
18
F
C
B♭
Though like the wan - - - der - er
20
F
C
Am7
The sun gone down,
8va

22
F C B♭ D m/F C C7
Dark - - ness be o - ver me, My rest a
(8va)
25
F C7
stone, Yet in my dreams I'd be Near - er, my
29
F/C C F C B♭add2
God, to thee, Near - er my God, to thee,
slight rit.
a tempo

Near - er to thee!

Moderato (♩ = c. 60-70)

There let the way ap - pear,

Steps un - to heav'n All that thou

43
C G G/F♯ G Am(add2)
send - - - est me, In mer - cy giv'n;
a tempo
46
B min C Maj7 C add2 D sus/G E min7/D G/D C G/B C
Angels to beck - on me Near - er, my
8va 15ma
f
8vb
51
G/D D G C Dsus2
God, to thee,
mf
8vb

56
D7
G
Cadd2
G
D7
Near - er, my God, to thee, Near - er
15ma
8va
mp
rit.
8vb
61
D7sus4/A D7
D7
G
CM9
GM9
to
thee!

"I Stand All Amazed" has been written in the key of A flat major. Play the A flat major scale below.

Once you feel comfortable playing the A flat major scale up and down one octave, try playing it 2, 3, and 4 octaves up and down the piano. As a fun exercise, try playing all of the scales and chords in every key signature by moving up in half steps to the right.

Ⓜ represents Major Chords

m represents minor Chords

d° represents diminished Chords

With each arrangement in this book, I have tried to create a different feeling or mood, not only with each arrangement, but within each individual verse. I began "I Stand All Amazed" as if I truly stand amazed, because I do, at every blessing I have received in my life. I stand all amazed at how much love and peace I feel from the Lord. Beginning at measure nine, I tried to create a feeling of uncertainty as to why I deserve to be so richly blessed. The uncertainty persists until measure 17 begins, at which point, a calm and reassuring feeling assures me of the Lord's love for me.

There are a few left hand patterns that are repeated throughout the arrangement. Practice playing these left hand patterns. For fun, try using these left hand patterns to arrange a hymn or two of your own. They are very easy to use and work well with almost every song.

When I teach my piano students about this left hand pattern, I refer to it as the "1 - 5 - 8 - 9 - 10" left hand pattern. Whatever note on which you start (e.g. in this case it is D flat) becomes the 1. Then you go to the fifth note above that (to the right, according to the major scale of the given key signature). You then proceed to the 8th (this is the octave and is the same not as the first note), then the 9th, and 10th notes from the note where you began. In the key of A flat major, using the example below, the notes are: D flat, A flat, D flat, E flat, and ending on F. For example, if you begin in the key of C, the notes will be C, G, C, D, and ending on E. Again, the pattern is "1 - 5- 8 - 9 - 10" and works in any key signature beginning on any note within the key.

This next pattern is very simple. Simply play the octave interval, and then play the 8th interval by itself. After that, you may either play the 10th interval, shown in the first measure, or the octave interval again played up an octave higher than the first, shown in the second measure. Once you have learned these patterns in this key, try playing them in every key moving up in half steps.

Try figuring out the left hand pattern shown below using the numbers "1 5 8 9 10"

I Stand All Amazed

Text and Music by Charles H. Gabriel, 1856-1932
ARR. BY JERALD SIMON

This can also be performed by a female voice. Sing it in your vocal range.

In awe and amazement (♩ = c. 65)

Lyrics:
I stand all a- mazed at the love Je- sus of- fers me,___ Con- fused at the grace that so ful- ly he prof- fers me.___ I trem- ble to know that for me he was cru- ci- fied,___ That for me, a sin- ner, he

Pedal ad lib. throughout

Vocal line (measures 18–21), *with feeling* ($\quarternote$ = c. 90):
suf - fered, he bled and died. Oh, it___ is won - der - ful that he should

Chords: E♭sus9/A♭   A♭susM9/D♭   A♭   E♭7sus4/A♭

Vocal line (measures 22–25):
care for me___ E-nough to die for me! Oh, it___ is won - der - ful, ___

Chords: E♭sus4   B♭min7/A♭   E♭sus/A♭   E♭sus7/D♭

Vocal line (measures 26–29), *Energetically* ($\quarternote$ = c. 112):
___ won - der - ful, to me! ___

Chords: D♭add2/E♭   A♭11   E♭/A♭

Chord symbols (measures 31–34): Ab11   Eb/Ab   Fm   Eb/F

Chord symbols (measures 35–39): Db11   Ebsus4   Eb   (♩ = c. 65) Ab

Lyrics (measures 40+): mar - vel that he would de - scend from his throne di - vine   To

Chord symbols (measures 40+): Ebm   Ebsus/Ab   Fm9/Ab

res- cue a soul so re- bel- ious and proud as mine, ___

That he should ex- tend his great love un- to such as I, ___ Suf- fi- cient to own, to re-

Lyrics:
deem, and to jus-ti-fy. Oh, it is won-der-ful that he should

care for me E-nough to die for me! Oh, it is won-der-ful,___

___ won-der-ful, to___ me!___

Lyrics:

I think of his hands pierced and blee-ding to pay the debt! Such mer-cy, such love and de-vo-tion can I_____ for-get? No, no, I will praise and a-dore at the mer-cy seat,_____ Until at the glo-ri-fied throne I kneel at his feet.

Oh, it___ is won-der-ful___ that he should care for me___ E-nough to

die for me! _____ Oh, it is

with feeling

rit.

a tempo   *a tempo*

($\quad$ = c. 95)

Energetically ($\quad$ = c. 112)

won-der-ful, _____ won-der-ful to me!

gradual cresc.

(♩ = c. 65)
117
F m
F m
B♭m11/D♭
E♭
A♭sus2
E♭/G
I stand all a-
(8va)
rit.
a tempo
124
A♭sus2/F
A♭sus2/D♭
D♭sus2/E♭
E♭7
A♭add2
mazed at the love Je-sus of - fers me!
rit.
128
A♭sus2/D♭
E♭add4
A♭add2
8va
15ma
pp

"Abide With Me" has been written in the key of E flat major. Play the E flat major scale below.

Once you feel comfortable playing the E flat major scale up and down one octave, try playing it 2, 3, and 4 octaves up and down the piano. As a fun exercise, try playing all of the scales and chords in every key signature by moving up in half steps to the right.

M represents Major Chords

m represents minor Chords

d° represents diminished Chords

On the second verse, I took the familiar right hand melody (shown below as the original right hand melody) and modified it by breaking the chords apart (shown below as the second verse right hand melody).

Play the original right hand melody of the hymn, "Abide With Me."

Play the right hand melody from the second verse (for fun, try to create your own right hand arrangement).

Arranging is as simple as taking the notes from a song or piece, changing the rhythm, and adding additional notes. The melody from the second verse is almost completely comprised of eighth notes. The melody is still present, but I have added additional notes in between the original melody line (the notes originally were half notes and quarter notes). Look carefully at both examples (the original right hand melody and the melody from the second verse). Discover the differences between the two and see if you can determine what chords I used to arrange the verse. As an example, in measure one from the second verse, you could think of the notes as a broken G minor chord in first inversion, or an E flat major seventh chord in second inversion. The notes to the E flat major seventh chord are E flat G B flat and D.

Abide With Me

Music by William H. Monk, 1823-1889
Text by Henry F. Lyte, 1793-1847

ARR. BY JERALD SIMON

This can also be performed by a female voice. Sing it in your vocal range.

Tenderly ♩ = 65

Lyrics:
A - bide with me! fast falls the e - ven - tide; The dark - ness deep - ens. Lord, with me a - bide! When oth - er help - ers fail and com - forts flee, Help of the help - less, oh, a -

Pedal ad-lib throughout

bide with me! Swift to its close ebbs

out life's lit - tle day. Earth's joys grow dim; its

glo - ries pass a - way. Change and de - cay in

all a-round I see; O thou who chang-est not, a-bide with _____ me!

I need thy

pres - ence ev - 'ry pass-ing hour. What but thy

45
A Maj7 E F♯min7 EM7 B E9 E Maj7/D♯
grace can foil the tempt-er's pow'r? Who, like thy -
8va 15ma
mp (gently)
50
C♯min7 G♯min7 C♯m7♯5/A B7 B7sus4/E G♯m7♯5/E B E/G♯
self, my guide and stay can be? Thru cloud and
p rit.
54
G♯m♭9♯5/A C♯m E/B B Bsus
sun - shine, Lord, a - bide with me!
8va 15ma
mf
8vb

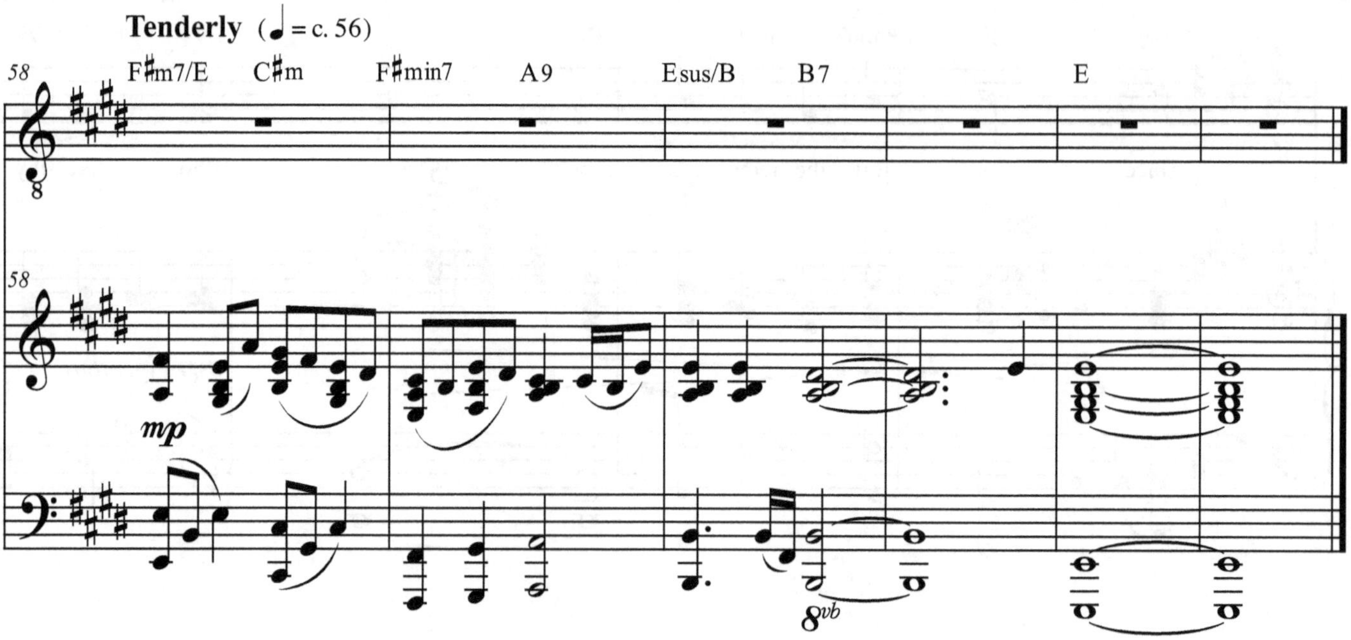
Tenderly (♩ = c. 56)
58
F♯m7/E C♯m F♯min7 A9 Esus/B B7 E
mp
8vb

"I Need Thee Every Hour" has been written in the key of G major. Play the G major scale below.

M represents Major Chords

m represents minor Chords

d° represents diminished Chords

Once you feel comfortable playing the G major scale up and down one octave, try playing it 2, 3, and 4 octaves up and down the piano. As a fun exercise, try playing all of the scales and chords in every key signature by moving up in half steps to the right.

Play the example below. This example shows the melody from the chorus of "I Need Thee Every Hour." The hymn is originally played in 3/4 time signature, but I wanted to create a feeling of longing by using 4/4 as the time signature. There is quite a bit of syncopation in this arrangement (where the off beat receives the accent). The "and 3" beat of most measures is tied. In the example below, I decided to use "D" as the primary note. D is the dominant note (the perfect 5th interval above G) in the key signature. In this example, notice how the other notes dance around the D, rocking from one note to another while continuing to return to the D. I wanted the D to be the center in this segment, symbolizing the Lord's consistent care and love for us, not only in our hour of need, but during every moment of our lives. I like to think that the D represents Diety.

I wanted to create the illusion that we need the Lord as little children need their parents. To create that sentiment, I decided to arrange "I Need Thee Every Hour" as a lullaby. Just as children long to hear their parents sing them to sleep, God longs to hear our prayers before we sleep. Here are the first few measures of the lullaby I created for this arrangement.

I Need Thee Every Hour/Lead Kindly Light

I Need Thee Every Hour - Music by Robert Lowry, 1826-1899, Text by Annie S. Hawks, 1835-1918
Lead Kindly Light - Music by John B. Dykes, 1823-1876, Text by John H. Newman, 1801-1890

ARR. BY JERALD SIMON

This can also be performed by a female voice. Sing it in your vocal range.

Tenderly ♩= 65

Lyrics:
I need thee ev-'ry hour, Most gra-cious Lord. _____ No
ten - der voice like thine Can peace __ a - fford. I need thee, oh, I
need thee; Ev - 'ry hour I need thee! Oh, bless me now, my Sav - ior I

Pedal ad-lib throughout

Beautifully (♩ = c. 80)
16
G D7 D7 D7 A7/G F♯m
come to thee.
8va
mp
a tempo
22
A sus4/D Cadd2 A7/G F♯m A sus4/E
(8va)
mf
27
Cadd2 D7sus4 D7 G/D
Lead, kind - ly Light, a-mid th'en
rit.
a tempo

Lyrics (vocal line):

m. 32 (Cadd2/G C G D D7 G): cir-cling gl-oom;___ Lead thou me on!___ The night is dark, and I am

m. 36 (Cadd2 C/G G G/D D Gadd2 C), Moderato (♩ = c. 90): far from ho-me;___ Lead thou me o - n.___

m. 41 (Dsus/G C G): I need thee, ev - 'ry

Left hand crosses over right hand for additional notes played in the right hand.

45
C
hour; St-ay thou near
49
G
D
G
by Temp - ta - tions lose their pow'r When
53
Dadd2/A
F♯m7/A
Dsus
D
Gadd2
thou art nigh. I need thee; oh, I
rit.
a tempo

need thee; Ev' - ry___ hour___ I need thee!

Oh, bless_____ me___ now, my Sav - - - ior.

I come_____ to___

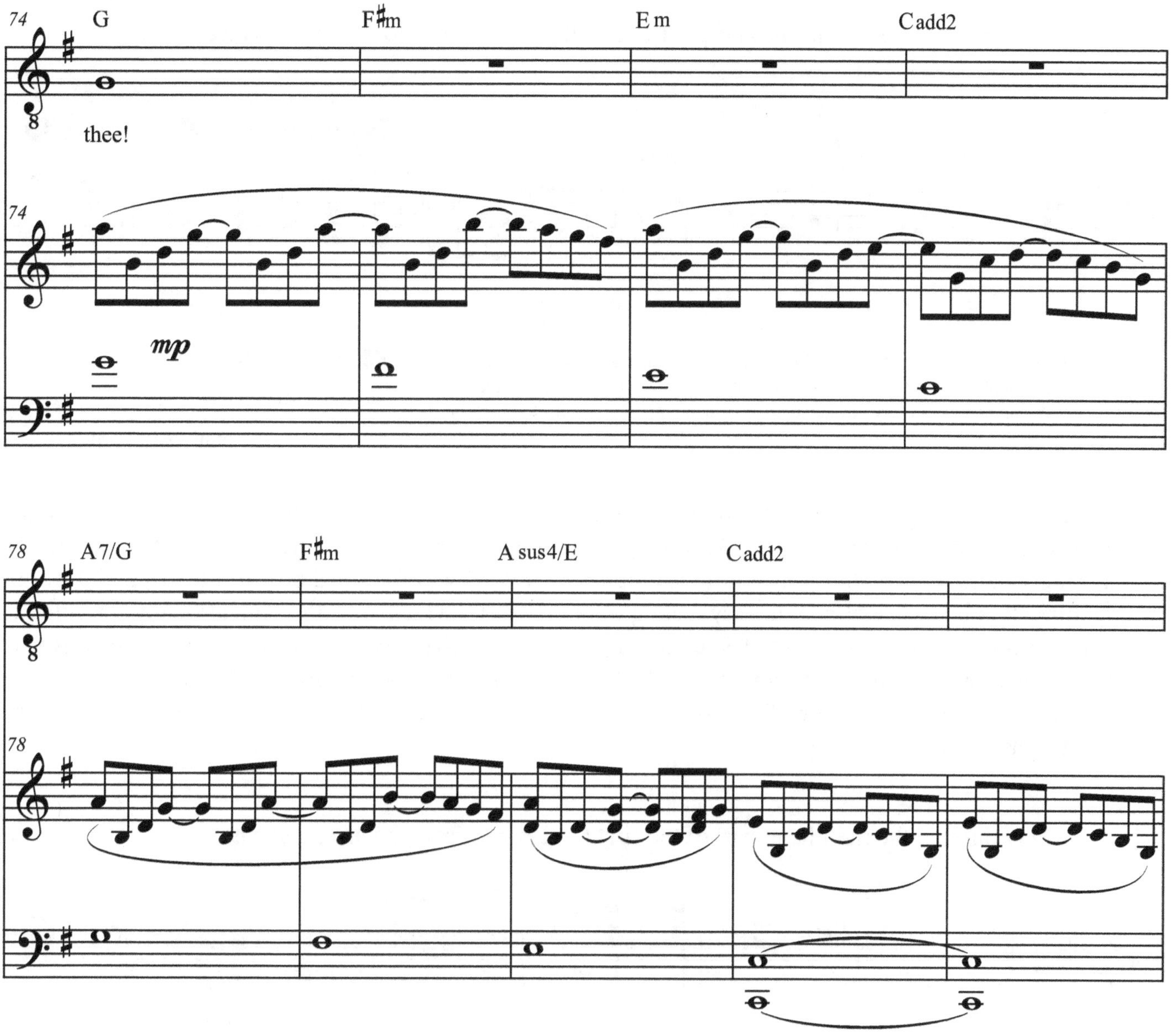
74
G
F♯m
E m
Cadd2
thee!
74
mp
78
A 7/G
F♯m
A sus4/E
Cadd2
78

"More Holiness Give Me" has been written in the key of D major. Play the D major scale below.

Once you feel comfortable playing the D major scale up and down one octave, try playing it 2, 3, and 4 octaves up and down the piano. As a fun exercise, try playing all of the scales and chords in every key signature by moving up in half steps to the right.

Ⓜ represents Major Chords

m represents minor Chords

d° represents diminished Chords

I changed the time signature from 4/4 to 6/8 time signature. The original version of the hymn shows triplets and is taken much slower (about 46 - 52 beats per minute). By having the hymn in 6/8 time signature, the natural accent is off beat and puts a unique emphasis on what was the third beat in the original 4/4 time signature. This brings an almost uneasy feeling of discomfort - which was done intentionally. I wanted to portray musically that although we desire more holiness in our lives, we often feel as if we are unworthy of His holiness. I wanted the arrangement to feel a little bit rushed as if we cannot wait for the Lord to give us more of His holiness, but then realizing that true holiness cannot be given away, it must be earned by living lives of righteousness.

Play through the right hand part of the first 6 measures from the arrangement.

This next example shows measures 7 - 12. Measure seven is a continuation of the previous style, mainly playing the octave chords. A suspended 4th has been added (the fourth note above A was added to the major octave chord in measure 7). Beginning in measure 8, the top note descends simply and cautiously, while following the major scale. The next measures, 9 - 12, are broken chords. I merely used the same chords from the previous example, but broke them apart and added an accent to bring out the melody.

Whenever you arrange a song, it is almost always in your best interest to have the melody on top. I tell students to play the melody with their pinkies and "fill in the notes below" using broken and blocked chords. If you play a C major chord in first inversion, the C will be on top, the G will be in the middle, and the E will be on the bottom. The C receives the attention. What if you played the same chord, but added an A or B below the C? You would produce either the C major sixth or the C major seventh chord. Try it out.

More Holiness Give Me

Music and Text by Philip Paul Bliss, 1838-1876
ARR. BY JERALD SIMON

This can also be performed by a female voice. Sing it in your vocal range.

With Feeling (♪ = c. 54)

Tenor

More ho - li - ness give me, More striv - ings with - i - n,

Pedal ad-lib throughout

More pa - tience in suf - fring, More sor - row for sin,

More faith in my sav - ior, More sense of his care,

More joy in his ser - vice, More pur-pose in prayer.

More grat - i - tude give me, More trust in the Lor - d.

More pride in his glo - ry, More hope in his word,

25 Dsus ... G ... Bm ... Asus4/D ... DMaj7/C#

More tears for his sor-rows, More pain at his grief,

f

29 Bm ... D/A ... Dsus/G ... G ... Asus ... A ... Dadd2/G

More meek-ness in tri-al, More praise for re-lief.

33 Dadd2 ... Eadd2 ... Asus/D Dm♭9#5 ... GM7 ... A

More pur-i-ty give me, More strength to o'er-co-me.

mp

mf

8va

Lyrics:

More freedom from earth-stains, More longing for home.

More fit for the king-dom, More used would I be,

More bless-ed and ho-ly - More, Sav-ior, like thee.

Lyrics under the vocal line: More ho-li-ness give me!

"If You Could Hie to Kolob," or "I Heard the Voice of Jesus," had been written in the key of G Major (E minor). Review the G Major scale from the first hymn in this book ("For the Beauty of the Earth").

"If You Could Hie to Kolob" was originally an English melody, and is known by many titles throughout the world. Each area has its own title and lyrics. The music is enchanting and has a bitter sweet mood about it.

In this arrangement, I change keys by going from a minor to a major key. The hymn begins in the key of G Major, but it is actually the key of E minor, which is the relative minor to G Major. I wanted to change the mood of the hymn to give it a happy and bright sounding feeling and changed from E minor to E Major, Then we change keys again from E Major to B Major. Near the end of the hymn, we return to the relative minor. Since we are now in the key of B Major, the relative minor is G sharp minor.

You should be able to play any song in a minor or major key signature. If it is major and you want to turn it into a minor sounding arrangement, simply flat the 3rd, 6th, and 7th notes from the major scale. If the song is in a minor key signature and you want to turn it into a major sounding song, simply sharp the 3rd, 6th, or 7th notes from the minor scale of the given key signature. Try it! It's very easy to do because you are playing the same notes from the song or piece and you are only changing the 3rd, 6th, and 7th notes from the major or minor scale. Here is an excerpt from the arrangement where one note was used after every other note. In this case, G is the main note I chose to rock back and forth to as a type of pivot point.

Play this example from the song.

Here we changed from E minor to E major. Play the example below. To create the major feel, I sharped the 3rd, 6th, and 7th notes from the E minor scale to create the E major key signature.

If You Could Hie to Kolob

This can also be performed by a female voice. Sing it in your vocal range.

Thought Provoking ♩ = 65

Music English melody
Text by William W. Phelps, 1792-1872
ARR. BY JERALD SIMON

Pedal ad-lib throughout

gradual crescendo

Lyrics:
If you could hie to Ko-lob In the twin-kling of an eye, And then con-tin-ue on-ward With that same speed to fly, Do you think that you could ev-er, Through all e-ter-ni-

12
Dsus4 D Cadd2 E7/D Em D/F♯
ty Find out the gen - er - a - - - tion Where
12
f
15
G Am11/C C/D Em Cadd2/G Em
Gods be - gan to be. Or see the grand be -
15
mp
20
C D G Dsus4 Cadd2
gin - ning, Where space did not ex - tend? Or view the last cre -
20

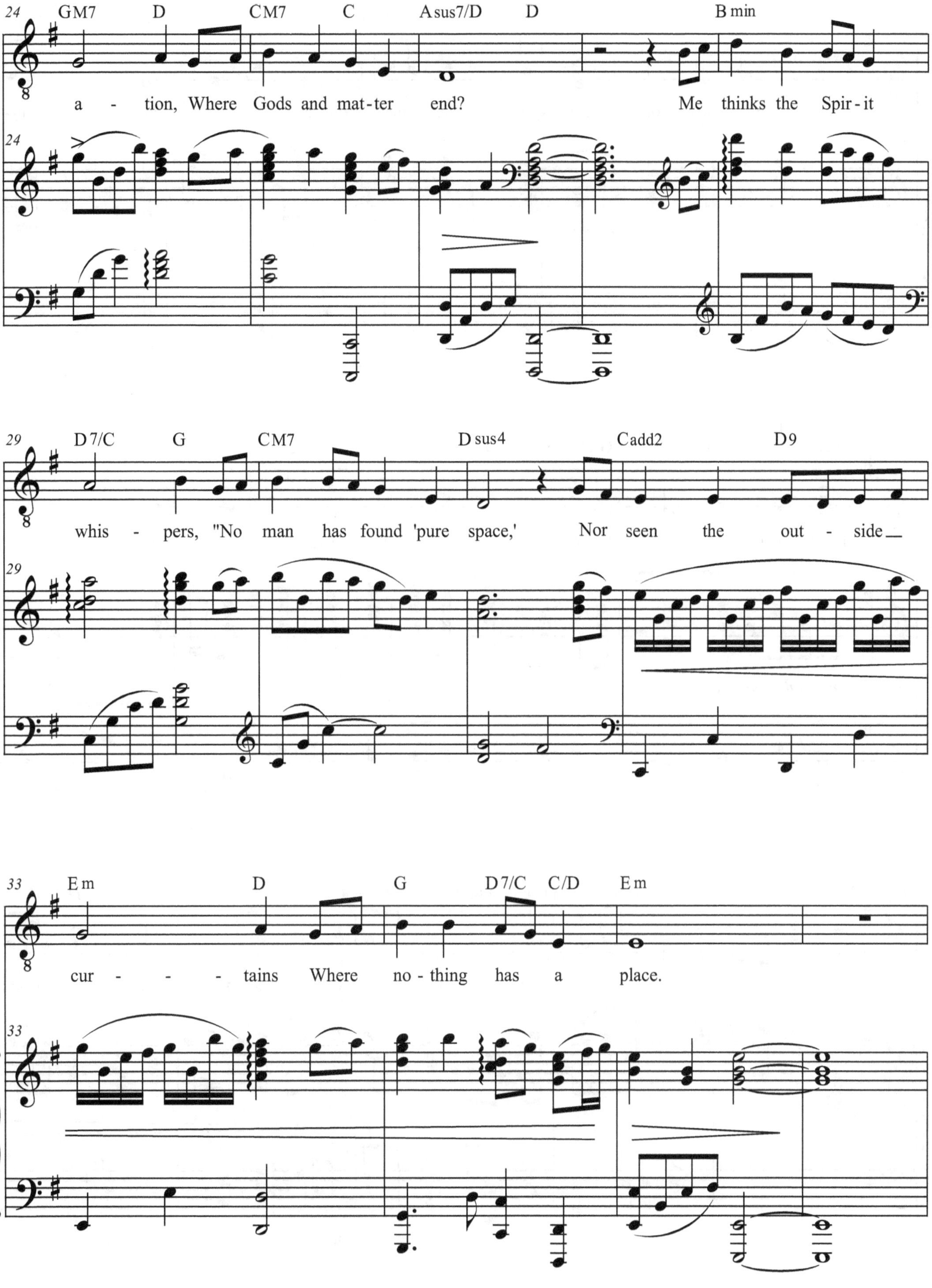
GM7 D CM7 C Asus7/D D B min
a - tion, Where Gods and mat-ter end? Me thinks the Spir-it
D7/C G CM7 D sus4 Cadd2 D9
whis - pers, "No man has found 'pure space,' Nor seen the out - side
Em D G D7/C C/D Em
cur - - - tains Where no-thing has a place.

The Works of God continue, And worlds and lives abound; Improvement and progression Have one eternal round. There is no end to matter; There is no end to space; There

51
Cadd2 E7/D Em D/F♯ D
is no end to spir - - - - - it; There
f
53
G D7/C C/D Em E/B E/B E C♯m
is no end to race. There is no end to
f
8vb
58
E/B B7 C♯m B7 E/G♯ A Bsus4 B C♯m C♯min7/B
vir - tue; There is no end to might There is no end to
8vb

wis - dom; There is no end to light. There is no end to

un - ion; There is no end to youth; youth; There is no end to___

priest - - hood; There is no end to truth. There

75
D♯sus/G♯ E C♯sus/F♯ B F♯ G♯m F♯ B C♯m F♯sus F♯ B/F♯
is no end to glo - ry; there is no end to love; There
mp
79
E9 C♯min F♯/A♯ B/D♯ C♯7 F♯ B/D♯F♯/C♯ B C♯m11/E E/F♯ G♯m
is no end to be - ing; There is no death a bove.
gradual crescendo
mp
8vb
83
G♯m B G♯m C♯m7/E D♯m7/F♯ B E M7
There is no end to glo - ry; There is no end to
8vb
8vb

87
F♯sus4
F♯
E
F♯9
love;
There is no end to
90
F♯/A♯
E Maj7
F♯sus
F♯
G♯m7/B
be - - - ing; There is no death a - bove.
8va
15ma
rit.
8vb

I want to thank you for playing these hymn arrangements. I love playing hymns as well as embellishing and arranging them because it is a way for me to share my love of the gospel of Jesus Christ with others. As I arrange hymns, I love thinking about the emotions I hope to convey through the arrangement. I often use the words of the hymns to dictate how I will arrange certain sections. This allows me to play certain parts in major or minor key signatures or various modes. I have tried to arrange each of these in an exultant way, which is why I have titled this book, "Hymns of Exaltation." I hoped to convey the feeling of longing to return back to our Heavenly home above.

I want to end this book with my testimony of my Savior, Jesus Christ.

I love my Savior. I am so grateful for Jesus Christ. I know He is God's son, and the only perfect being to walk the face of this earth. I know Jesus can lead me and guide me, and I will strive to follow Him. I can turn to Him when I need help or if I lose my way. I need my Savior, Jesus Christ, in my life - every minute of every day. He is my brother. I look up to Him, and I am striving to live His teachings and be more Christ-like.

I am eternally thankful for the atonement and how Jesus Christ overcame death - both physical and spiritual death. Jesus suffered for my sins. He is perfect and took upon himself my imperfections. He suffered not only for my spiritual pains and sins, but he also suffered the physical pains of every heartache, sickness, physical, mental, or emotional suffering I have ever or will ever experience in life. He took upon himself my infirmities so He could strengthen me, even in spite of my weaknesses. He will never lead me astray. He knows my weaknesses and he knows my strengths.

Jesus lifts me when I have fallen. He strengthens me when I am weak. He brings me light when I wander in the darkness. He comforts and cradles me when I am broken and hurt. He wipes away my tears when I experience the sorrows of mortality. I am so grateful to my Heavenly Father and my Savior, Jesus Christ, for all they have done and continually do for me.

I know our Heavenly Father sent us here to earth as part of His eternal plan of happiness. I am so grateful for the gospel of Jesus Christ and its goodness in my life. Living by the teachings in the scriptures helps me focus my faith and testimony on everything that is noteworthy, praiseworthy, and edifying. The gospel of Jesus Christ, the scriptures, and the commandments of God mean everything to me. It changes the way I see the world, the thoughts I think, the words I speak, and every choice I make. It impacts everything around me, because it changes everything within me.

I hope we can all focus on the things of eternity. If we will think about our heavenly home above with God, Jesus Christ, and the Holy Ghost - in addition to our family, friends, and loved ones from the past, present, and future, then we will learn to see with eternal eyes. We will be able to see things as they really are and should be. We will be able to look past the temptations and sorrows that surround us, and we will instead focus on faith and our eternal future with our Heavenly Father.

God loves us. We are His children and we are all brothers and sisters. As we serve each other and help one another overcome our own natural weaknesses, then we can focus on being and becoming who our Heavenly Father wants us to be.

I'm grateful for each of you. Do your best and be your best. God loves you and so do I!

- JERALD SIMON

A Few Additional New Age Music Books for Piano Teachers and Parents of Piano Students

If you enjoyed these hymn arrangements, I think you will also enjoy working through contemporary classical/new age and cinematic sounding piano solos from my other books.

I teach about composing new age music in my Essential Piano Exercises Course (https://www. essentialpianoexercises.com/course). Within the course, I am uploading video lessons for every exercise and piano solo from each of the current books within the series. More books are being added to the series. I'd love to have you join the **Essential Piano Exercises Course**.

After you have had a chance to play through the hymn arrangements from this book, I'd love to have you film yourself playing one of these hymns. You can share your video of you playing/singing one of these hymn arrangements solo on social media, and I'd love to have you tag me in the video so I can see your great performance (@jeraldsimon). I always enjoy watching piano students perform music I have composed or arranges, and would love to see your progress!

Here is a URL link to a playlist on my YouTube channel that has music videos for every hymn arrangement from this book:

youtube.com/jeraldsimon

If you enjoyed these piano solos, I think you will enjoy the following additional books I have written.

Here are some titles to other new age music books and albums I have composed that you may enjoy:

Adventure Awaits - https://tinyurl.com/adventure-awaits-jerald-simon
Wintertide - https://tinyurl.com/wintertide-by-jerald-simon
Sweet Melancholy - https://tinyurl.com/sweet-melancholy
Sea Fever - https://tinyurl.com/sea-fever-by-Jerald-Simon
Triumphant - https://tinyurl.com/triumphant-by-jerald-simon
Castles in the Sky - https://tinyurl.com/castles-in-the-sky
Hymns of Exaltation - https://tinyurl.com/hymns-of-exaltation
Peace and Serenity - https://tinyurl.com/peace-and-serenity

Every so often, I try to release a new album/music book featuring meditation or relaxation music - all of which fall under the new age style of music. Most of these albums and books feature fully orchestrated pieces and not just piano solos. Some feature nature sounds, ocean waves, waterfalls, wind, crickets, or other soothing nature sounds and effects that have been combined with music. Many of these compositions are meditation/relaxation themed because they have been composed with the intention of helping the listener be comforted.

You can listen to my music on Spotify, Pandora, iTunes, Amazon, and of course, you can watch all of my music videos and additional piano lesson tutorials on my YouTube channel.

A Few Additional Ideas for Piano Teachers and Parents of Piano Students

You can visit this link to read the original blog post from which this presentation was created: (https://www.musicmotivation.com/blog/don-t-teach-music-theory-unless-you-teach-the-practical-application).

In the blog post, I talked specifically about 10 steps to begin teaching the practical application of music theory so students know their theory inside and out. I thought I would share the 10 steps here from the blog post:

Before any piano student plays their piece, I believe they should be able to do the following (this is what I try to have my students do with their music):

1. Tell their music teacher the key signature and time signature.

2. Identify all of the sharps or flats in the key signature.

3. Play all of the intervals created from the major key signature of the piece they are playing - this is more for piano students and possibly guitar students, as many instruments only allow one note at a time. If the student is younger or new to their instrument, they can play the intervals created from the pentascales or five note scales created from the first five notes of the major or minor scales.

4. Play through the major scale of the key signature of the piece at least 1-2 octaves up and down the piano (parallel and or contrary motion). If the student is younger or new to their instrument, as stated before, they can play the pentascales, or five note scales created from the first five notes of the major or minor scales.

5. Play what I refer to as the "Essential Piano Exercises" from each key signature. (In the blog post I show an example from the key of C major from my book "Essential Piano Exercises" - Intervals, Scales, and Chords in all Keys and in all Inversions - a 288 page book with all intervals, scales, and simple triads and 6th and 7th chords in all keys and inversions).

These are the other 5 steps:

Once a student can do the above five essential "getting started steps" in any given key signature (and many times I will do the following steps even if they can't do the above steps in every key signature), I then challenge them to do the following five essential "music theory application steps."

1. Once the student has learned and perfected the piece, ask him or her to take the song up half a step and down half a step. In the beginning, this is a good start. Later on, when they are better able to do so, have the student play the piece in any key signature. Start with simple pieces like "Mary Had a Little Lamb" and "Twinkle, Twinkle, Little Star." Have the students try playing these in all key signatures.

2. Ask the student to come up with at least 5-10 variations or arrangements of their piece.

3. Ask the student to compose 3 or 4 motifs (or single melodic line or phrase), and then put them together. This can be the beginning of creating a simple piece. I have students begin using scales and skipping notes here and there. We then have them take a simple pattern created from the notes of the major scale (1 2 3 4 5 6 7 8).

4. Ask the student to "Play a Rainbow." When I say this to students, I then begin to ask them to "play" anything. I may say: "Play me a shadow," "Play me a swing set," or "Play me a thunderstorm," "Play me a puddle, a rock, a tree, a meadow, a light, etc.". The sky is the limit. I first begin with tangible objects and eventually move on to intangible ideas and concepts: "Play me loneliness," "Play me disturbed, agitated, angered, humbled, pensive, etc.". Again, the sky is the limit. It is wonderful to see what students can create, even if they don't know all the rules of composition or terminology. Everyone has music within them.

5. I have students begin notating their music. I enjoy and prefer Finale, but that is because I have used it for so long and am familiar with it. There are many great programs available. After we have their music put down on paper, I then export the music from Finale as a midi file and open the midi file in Logic Pro. We then begin having them add additional instruments so they can create background tracks (this is how I create all of my weekly "**Cool Songs**" from my **COOL SONGS Series** (you can learn more about my COOL SONGS Series at this link: https://musicmotivation.com/coolsongs/). The students then have a PDF copy of their composition and an MP3 "minus track" to accompany them as they play. Talk about music motivation!

These are the books included in the COOL SONGS Series: https://musicmotivation.com/coolsongs/ -

The Apprentice Stage - The Maestro Stage - The Virtuoso Stage

COOL SONGS for COOL KIDS (Primer Level) by Jerald Simon
COOL SONGS for COOL KIDS (book 1) by Jerald Simon
COOL SONGS for COOL KIDS (book 2) by Jerald Simon
COOL SONGS for COOL KIDS (book 3) by Jerald Simon
COOL SONGS that ROCK! (book 1) by Jerald Simon
COOL SONGS that ROCK! (book 2) by Jerald Simon

Join the **Essential Piano Exercises Course** by Jerald Simon
https://www.essentialpianoexercises.com

Gain lifetime access to the PDF books listed below (which also includes video piano lesson tutorials where Jerald Simon demonstrates examples from the books and gives piano pointers, tips to try, and the practical application of music theory). Jerald demonstrates how to use the music theory to arrange and compose music of your own!

This course features pre-recorded video lessons so you can watch and learn how to play the piano at your convenience. You choose when and where you learn to play the piano.

Join the **Essential Piano Exercises Course** and receive the following PDF books along with access to the monthly video lesson taught by Jerald Simon for a one time payment of $199.95.

youtube.com/jeraldsimon

I upload new videos on Wednesdays, and Fridays on my YouTube channel, **youtube.com/jeraldsimon**. I have a few different playlists filled with great content for beginning - advanced piano students. The videos are geared for everyone from brand new piano students to music majors, professional pianists, and piano teachers of all skill levels.

There are three main playlists for my **free on-line piano lessons.** I do offer in person piano lessons, Zoom/FaceTime piano lessons, and step by step piano lesson packages you can purchase and watch at home (https://www.musicmotivation.com/pianolessons), but the ones listed below are FREE to everyone who subscribes to my YouTube channel:

1. **PIANO FUNdamentals** (emphasis on the word FUN!)
2. **5 Minute Piano Lessons with Jerald Simon** (sponsored by Music Motivation®)
3. **Theory Tip Tuesday Piano Lessons**

I frequently release new videos. Some are piano lessons, and others are filmed recordings of workshops, masterclasses, or concerts. I also have these additional types of videos on my YouTube channel:

a. Meditation/Relaxation Music Composed by Jerald Simon
b. Hymn Arrangements by Jerald Simon
c. Motivational Messages by Jerald Simon
d. Motivational Poetry by Jerald Simon
e. Theory Tip Tuesday (FREE Weekly Piano Lesson Videos) by Jerald Simon
f. Cool Songs by Jerald Simon (musicmotivation.com/coolsongs)
g. Assemblies, Workshops, Firesides, and more...

Let me know if you have a tutorial you'd like me to come out with to better help you learn the piano. I'm happy to help in any way I can and love hearing feedback from others about what they personally are looking for in piano lesson videos to help them learn to play the piano better. I primarily focus on music theory, improvisation/arranging, and composition. I refer to these as **THEORY THERAPY, INNOVATIVE IMPROVISATION, and CREATIVE COMPOSITION**.

I have also produced hundreds of COOL SONGS that teach students music theory the fun way. If you'd like to learn more about the COOL SONGS, that I composed to motivate my own piano students, or if you would like to purchase the COOL SONGS series featuring the music/books, simply visit musicmotivation.com/coolsongs to be taken to the page on my website that explains a little more about the COOL SONGS. You can also watch piano video tutorial lessons featuring 85 of the 200 + COOL SONGS (youtube.com/jeraldsimon). Let me know what you think. I'd love your feedback about the music. It helps me as I compose more COOL SONGS to motivate more piano students. I'm excited to have you watch my free video piano lessons on YouTube.com/jeraldsimon.

$\mathcal{L}$earn more about
JERALD SIMON

Visit https://www.musicmotivation.com/jeraldsimon

"My purpose and mission in life is to motivate myself and others through my music and writing, to help others find their purpose and mission in life, and to teach values and encourage everyone everywhere to do and be their best." - Jerald Simon

First and foremost, Jerald is a husband to his beautiful wife, Zanny, and a father to his wonderful children. Jerald Simon is the founder of **Music Motivation®** (musicmotivation.com), a company he formed to provide music instruction through workshops, giving speeches and seminars, concerts and performances in the field of music and motivation. He is a composer, author, poet, and Music Mentor/piano teacher (primarily focusing his piano teaching on music theory, improvisation, composition, and arranging). Jerald loves spending time with his wife, Zanny, and their children. In addition, he loves music, teaching, speaking, performing, playing sports, exercising, reading, writing poetry and self help books, and gardening.

Jerald Simon is the founder of **Music Motivation®** and focuses on helping piano students and piano teachers learn music theory, improvisation, and composition. He refers to these areas as: **Theory Therapy™, Innovative Improvisation™, and Creative Composition™.** Simon is an author and composer and has written 30 music books featuring almost 300 original compositions, 15 albums (you can listen to Jerald's music on Pandora, Spotify, iTunes, Amazon, and all online music stations. Jerald's books and CDs are also available from Amazon, Wal-Mart.com, Barnes and Noble and all major retail outlets). He has published three motivational poetry books featuring over 400 original poems (poetrythatmotivates.com), and is the creator of the best-selling **Cool Songs Series** (musicmotivation.com/coolsongs), the best-selling **Essential Piano Exercises Series** (essentialpianoexercises.com) and Essential Piano Lessons for piano students (essentialpianolessons.com). He has also created **Essential Piano Teachers** for piano teachers (essentialpianoteachers.com). You can watch Jerald's videos on his YouTube channel at: youtube.com/jeraldsimon. Listen to Jerald's music on all streaming sites and his podcast, **Music, Motivation, and More – The Positivity Podcast** with Jerald Simon on all podcast platforms.

In 2008, Jerald began creating his Cool Songs to help teach music theory – the FUN way, by putting FUN back into theory FUNdamentals. Jerald has also filmed hundreds of piano lesson video tutorials on his YouTube page (youtube.com/jeraldsimon). In addition to music books and albums, he is the author/poet of **"The As If Principle"** (motivational poetry), and the books **"Perceptions, Parables, and Pointers," "Motivation in a Minute,"** and **"Who Are You?"**.

SPECIALTIES:

Composer, Author, Poet, Music Mentor, Piano Teacher (jazz, music theory, improvisation, composition, arranging, etc.), Motivational Speaker, and Life Coach. Visit **https://www.musicmotivation.com/**, to book Jerald as a speaker/performer. Visit **https://www.musicmotivation.com/** to print off FREE piano resources for piano teachers and piano students.

Book me to speak/perform for your group or for a concert or performance:

jeraldsimon@musicmotivation.com - **(801)644-0540** - https://www.musicmotivation.com/

www.ingramcontent.com/pod-product-compliance
Lightning Source LLC
LaVergne TN
LVHW061340060426
835511LV00014B/2023